Life in ...

A Clearing in a Forest

First published in the UK in 2000 by
Belitha Press Limited
London House, Great Eastern Wharf,
Parkgate Road, London SW11 4NQ

Editor: Russell McLean
Designer: Louise Morley
Picture researcher: Sally Morgan
Educational consultant: Emma Harvey

ISBN 1 84138 169 1

Printed in Singapore

British Library Cataloguing in Publication Data
for this book is available from the British Library.

10 9 8 7 6 5 4 3 2 1

Picture acknowledgements:
Steve Austin/Papilio: front cover c, 19tr. Ian Beames/Ecoscene: 25b.
Frank Blackburn/Ecoscene: front cover tl, 7b, 11, 12b, 16t, 17, 18, 22t,
24-25, 26t, 27b, 27t. Andrew Brown/Ecoscene: 6, 15l, 23r, 24c.
Anthony Cooper/Ecoscene: 21t. Chinch Gryniewicz/Ecoscene: 10b, 13b, 15r,
23tl, 29b. Angela Hampton/Ecoscene: 25t. J. Howard/Sylvia Cordaiy
Photo Library: 14b. Leaper/Ecoscene: 28b. Sally Morgan/Ecoscene: front & back
cover background, 7t, 13t, 16b, 28-29. Papilio: 14t, 17t, 20c, 22b. Robin Redfern/
Ecoscene: 10t, 19c, 26b. David Saunders/Sylvia Cordaiy Photo Library:
front cover br, 3, 11b. Barrie Watts: front cover cl, 7c, 12t, 19b, 20-21.

Words in **bold** are explained in the glossary on page 30.

Life in ...

A Clearing
in a Forest

Sally Morgan

Belitha Press

Contents

What is a forest?

A forest is a place where trees grow closely together. The animals and plants in this book live in **temperate** forests in North America or Europe. Temperate regions have **seasons**.

Summers in a temperate forest are short and warm. Winters are cold. Rain falls all the year round. Most of the forest trees are **deciduous**. This means they drop their leaves in the autumn and grow new ones in the spring.

◀ The sweet chestnut tree produces nuts. Each nut grows inside a spiny case. Many animals eat the nuts.

Many different animals live in the forest. Birds and insects fly among the leaves. Larger animals, such as foxes and badgers, move around on the forest floor. Beetles, worms and other small animals live on the bark of trees and in the **leaf litter** on the ground. Some of the animals only visit the forest during the warmer parts of the year.

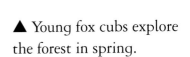

▲ Young fox cubs explore the forest in spring.

◀ In autumn, the trees and **shrubs** are covered in berries.

The clearing

A clearing is a gap in the forest where there are no trees. It is an open, sunny place where grasses and tall shrubs grow. At the edge are tall flowering plants. The animals that live in the clearing are different from those that live in the forest.

Many different types of grasses grow in the sunny clearing. In summer, the grasses grow quickly, forming a thick mass of green leaves. In winter, the grasses die. Tall plants, such as bracken, grow at the edge of the clearing.

In the forest, the branches and leaves of tall trees form a roof, or **canopy**, over the ground. They block the light from plants that grow beneath the trees.

Smaller trees and shrubs grow under the trees. They form the shrub layer. Birds nest in their dense branches.

The forest floor is covered by fallen leaves and twigs. Large logs are covered in mosses, **ferns** and **fungi**. Low-growing plants, such as brambles and ivy, creep along the ground.

Forest canopy

Shrub layer

Forest floor

Clearing

9

A roof over the forest

The tree branches form a roof over the forest. This is called the canopy. Above the trees it is sunny and windy. Beneath the canopy it is shady and much cooler.

▲ The grey squirrel eats nuts, seeds and fruits.

The leaves of the trees are broad, but thin. They are the right shape to capture sunlight, which the trees need to make food. But the leaves block much of the sun from smaller plants growing beneath the canopy.

Many animals live in the canopy. Squirrels leap from tree to tree in search of nuts and fruits. Insects munch holes in leaves, **shoots** and tree trunks. Hunters live in the canopy too. Spiders spin webs to trap insects. The sparrowhawk and kestrel are **birds of prey** which eat smaller animals.

◀ The canopy of the forest forms a green roof.

▼ Sparrowhawks build their nests high in the trees. From here they can watch over the forest, looking for prey.

Birds nest in the trees. Each bird has its favourite nesting site. Woodpeckers and owls look for holes in tree trunks. Blackbirds live in forks in the branches. Crows nest high in the canopy, well away from other birds.

◀ Woodpeckers live in holes in tree trunks. They search for insects under the bark.

The forest floor

Many small animals hide among the fallen leaves and twigs on the forest floor. Insects, earthworms and other creatures tunnel through the soil. Most of them stay hidden or are too small to see.

These animals play a vital role in the forest – they break down **dung**, dead animals and dead plants. This is called **recycling**. It begins when animals such as beetles and ants chew leaves into tiny pieces.

▲ Toadstools are fungi. These fly agarics are **poisonous**.

Then **fungi** and **bacteria** begin to rot down the pieces into a black, crumbly material called **humus**. This releases **nutrients**, which the plants take in through their roots. Plants use the nutrients to grow. Without them, the forest plants would die.

◀ This stag beetle is looking for dead leaves to chew.

Fungi are made up of tiny threads called **hyphae**. The hyphae grow through the soil, forming a network of threads. In autumn, some of the threads grow above ground. They form a **fruiting body**, which we call a toadstool or a mushroom. Each fruiting body releases millions of tiny **spores**. Some of the spores will land on a bare patch of soil and grow into a new fungus.

▼ Small plants called mosses grow in damp, shady places on the forest floor.

▲ In autumn, clumps of toadstools appear around rotting tree stumps.

The edge of the clearing

Trees surround the forest clearing. They provide shelter from the wind. In the clearing, the air is still. The sun warms the ground.

Tall plants, such as foxgloves and willowherbs, live under the trees at the edge of the clearing. Here it is sheltered, but not too sunny.

▲ Lady's slipper orchids live under the canopy of the forest and at the edge of the clearing.

Climbing plants grow up trees and over **shrubs**. They include brambles and ivy. These plants start life as tiny **seedlings** on the ground. As they grow, they use other plants for support, twining their shoots around the trees and shrubs. In this way, the climbing plants reach the sunlight.

◄ The trunk of this tree is almost completely covered with ivy. Birds may hide their nests among the dense shoots.

14

There are large **ferns**, such as bracken, at the edge of the clearing. Ferns like damp and shady places. They live near the trees, rather than in the open. The large leaves of a fern are called **fronds**. Each frond grows from an underground stem called a **rhizome**.

◄ Brambles, red campions and ferns live in the shade beneath the trees.

▲ In spring, the fronds of a fern slowly uncurl as they grow.

Life in the clearing

▼ Butterflies visit flowers in the clearing to drink their sugary **nectar**.

The animals and plants that live in the clearing are different from those in the forest. In summer, the clearing is much sunnier and warmer than the forest. But in winter, it is much colder.

Grasses like the warm, dry clearing. The forest is too dark for them. Other plants produce brightly-coloured flowers in summer. The flowers attract hundreds of insects, such as bees and butterflies.

Some birds nest on the ground. They lay their eggs in a hollow among the grasses. The eggs are **camouflaged**, so they cannot be seen by other animals.

Deer come into the clearing to graze on the grasses. In early summer, the female deer leave their **fawns** in the safety of the tall grasses while they feed.

◀ The clearing is full of colourful flowers in summer.

Snakes and lizards like the sunny clearing too. In the morning, they sit in the sun, **absorbing** the heat. When their bodies have warmed up, they move off through the grass in search of small animals to eat.

▲ Every morning, adders lie in the sun to warm up.

▲ This woodcock is camouflaged — its feathers blend in with the colours of the woodland floor.

Night life

Many forest animals are **nocturnal**. This means they sleep in the day. As darkness falls, they creep into the forest to feed.

▶ This owl has caught a bird. The owl is returning to its nest to feed its chicks.

Large **mammals**, such as foxes and badgers, emerge from their underground homes at night. The badger lives in a deep burrow called a **sett**. Every night, it wanders along the same paths in the forest, hunting for nuts, berries, worms and voles. Hedgehogs, mice and voles search through the leaf litter, looking for juicy worms and slugs to eat.

▲ A family of badgers leaves its sett to hunt for food.

▲ This small bank vole has found a hazelnut on the forest floor.

▼ Stoats hunt at night. They eat mice and rabbits.

Only a few birds, such as owls and nightjars, fly by night. The owl has excellent hearing and sight. It can hear the faint sounds of mice, voles and insects as it flies silently over the clearing. Bats are nocturnal too. They sleep in the trees during the day and hunt for moths at night.

Spring arrives

In winter the trees are bare. You can see the shape of their branches clearly against the sky. The grasses and ferns have died back, and the floor is covered in rotting leaves.

▲ These sticky horse chestnut buds have begun to open.

One of the first signs of spring is the appearance of **catkins** on hazel and willow trees. Leaf **buds** on the trees begin to swell. Then the forest floor bursts into flower. Many plants survive the winter as bulbs in the ground. As soon as the temperatures start to rise, they send up new leaves.

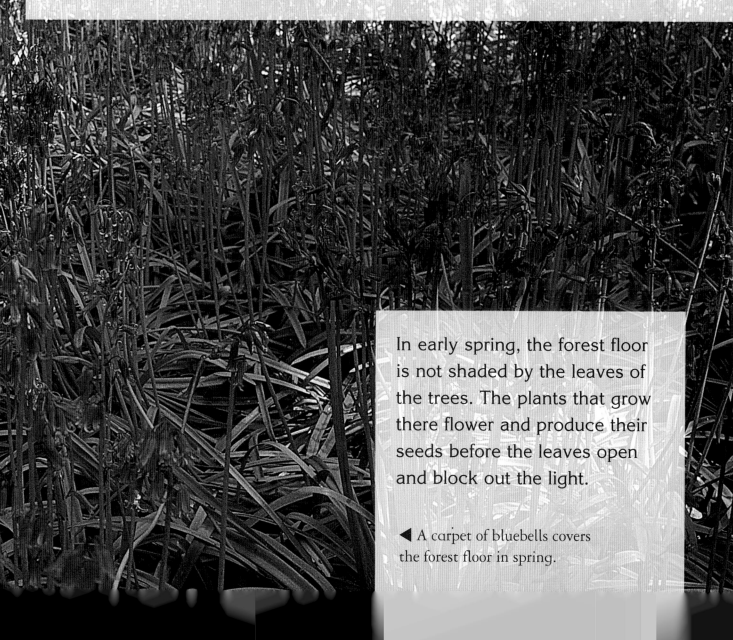

Many animals emerge from their winter resting places to find food. Birds return to the forest. They build nests and lay eggs in them. Foxes, deer and badgers give birth to young.

◀ A deer fawn hides in the long grass of the clearing.

In early spring, the forest floor is not shaded by the leaves of the trees. The plants that grow there flower and produce their seeds before the leaves open and block out the light.

◀ A carpet of bluebells covers the forest floor in spring.

Summer days

The end of spring is marked by the buds on the trees bursting into new leaves. The leaves shade the forest floor.

As more leaves open, the forest becomes darker. The trees produce flowers which set seed and produce fruits. The fruits are an important source of food for the forest animals.

▲ This pair of bullfinches have to work hard to keep their chicks fed.

▼ In summer, caterpillars turn into adult butterflies, such as this wood white butterfly.

For many animals, summer is a time for feeding. Armies of **caterpillars** munch through the leaves in the canopy. Within a few weeks, they **pupate**. This means they change into adult butterflies.

▲ Bees visit flowers to gather **pollen** and drink **nectar**. They take the pollen back to their hive.

Many animals search for food for their young. Badger and fox cubs grow quickly in summer. They need plenty to eat. Birds collect caterpillars and other insects for their fast-growing babies. The chicks grow feathers and take their first flight through the forest. Soon, they leave the nest for good. When there is plenty of food, some birds lay a second **clutch** of eggs.

▶ By late summer the forest is dark green. All the trees and shrubs are in leaf.

Preparing for winter

Autumn is a time of change. The trees prepare to drop their leaves. The leaves change colour – from green to brilliant yellow, orange and red – before they fall.

▲ Leaves of all colours cover the forest floor in autumn.

In summer, the tree roots soak up water in the soil. The water escapes from the leaves as **vapour**. In winter, the water in the ground may be frozen. The trees cannot afford to lose any water, so they drop their leaves.

The winter is too cold for some birds. In autumn, they fly hundreds of kilometres to places where the winter is warmer and there is plenty of food. This is called **migration**.

▲ Brown bears eat lots of food in autumn, before their long winter sleep.

Other animals, such as hedgehogs, squirrels and bears, spend the winter in a deep sleep called **hibernation**. In autumn, they eat nuts and fruits to build up their body fat. Then they creep into a warm, dry place such as a hole in a tree trunk or an underground burrow. By the time the first snow arrives, they are fast asleep.

▲ This bank vole is preparing for winter by eating berries.

A changing habitat

A forest clearing is changing all the time. Old trees die and topple over at its edge. New plants grow in the middle of the clearing.

The trees and shrubs in the forest produce seeds. These drop to the floor and are carried away by animals. Some seeds may land on patches of bare soil in the clearing.

▲ Most of these seedlings will die or be eaten by animals before they can grow into trees.

These seeds **germinate** and grow into **seedlings**. Most of them are eaten by voles and mice. Only one or two of the seedlings grow into adult trees, which cast shade over the surrounding plants. Plants that like sunny places are unable to survive. More trees appear. In time, trees and shrubs cover the clearing. It has become part of the forest again.

◄ Wood mice eat the tree seeds that fall to the forest floor.

▶ The jay buries nuts in the ground as a store of food for winter. Sometimes it forgets to return and the nuts grow into new trees.

A new clearing may form when an old tree dies and topples over. As the dead tree crashes to the ground, it pulls down other trees. Sometimes, strong winds and storms rip through the forest. They create new clearings by blowing over many trees.

◀ This large tree has fallen to the ground, creating a new clearing. The tree has pulled down smaller trees with it.

Saving the forests

In many places, forests are under threat. They are disappearing fast. Europe was once covered by dense forests. Only a few of these forests survive today.

Forests all over the world are being cut down to make space for farming, roads and new homes. Air **pollution** from cars and industry produces **acid rain**. Acid rain kills trees by damaging their leaves and roots.

Forests can be protected by turning them into nature reserves. People visit the reserves to learn about the woodland wildlife.

▲ Nest boxes help to replace nest sites that are lost when trees are cut down. This nest box is for an owl.

◄ Trees in the middle of this forest have been cut down to make way for a new road.

New forests can be created by planting trees on farmland. Damaged forests can be replanted. Some forests are **managed** to provide a never-ending supply of wood. Each year a different part of the forest is cut down. The trees are left to grow back again, so the wood can be harvested again in the future.

◄ This boy is planting a tree in a nature reserve.

Glossary

absorb To soak up.

acid rain Polluted rainwater that harms trees and plants.

bacteria Single-celled organisms that are too small to be seen with the naked eye.

bird of prey A bird that hunts other animals for food.

bud A leaf before it opens.

camouflage An animal's colour and patterns which help it to blend in with the background.

canopy The branches and leaves of trees.

caterpillar An early stage in the life of a butterfly or moth.

catkin A tuft of small flowers produced by shrubs such as willows and hazel.

clutch A group of eggs laid by one female bird.

deciduous Having leaves that fall in autumn.

dung Animal droppings.

fawn A baby deer.

fern A plant with feathery leaves and no flowers.

frond The leaf of a fern.

fruiting body The part of a fungus above ground, such as a mushroom or toadstool.

fungus (plural **fungi**) An organism that is neither animal nor plant. Most fungi are made up of tiny threads that grow through the soil.

germinate To begin to grow.

hibernation Spending the winter in a deep sleep.

humus Rotting leaves.

hyphae The underground threads of fungi.

leaf litter Dead leaves and twigs on the forest floor.

mammal A type of animal that feeds its young on milk.

managed Carefully looked after.

migration Moving or flying to a warmer place in winter.

nectar Sweet, sticky liquid made by flowers to attract insects.

nocturnal Active during the night.

nutrients Chemicals that plants and animals need for healthy growth.

poisonous Harmful.

pollen Yellow, powdery grains produced by the stamens (the male parts) of flowers.

pollution The release of harmful substances into the environment.

prey Animals that are killed by other animals for food.

pupate To change from a caterpillar into an adult butterfly.

recycling Turning waste material into something that can be used again.

rhizome An underground stem.

temperate Having seasons.

season One of the four parts of the year – spring, summer, autumn or winter.

seedling A very young plant.

sett The underground home of a family of badgers.

shoot A new growth from a plant.

shrub A small, tree-like bush.

spore A microscopic type of seed that will grow into a plant.

vapour A gas.

FURTHER READING

The following titles give more information about the plants and animals in this book. Some titles may be out of print, and only available in libraries.

Collins Complete British Wildlife Photoguide, Paul Sterry, Harper Collins, 1997.
Collins Field Guide: Trees of Britain and Northern Europe, Alan Mitchell, Harper Collins, 1978.
Collins Wild Guide: Birds of Britain and Ireland, Peter Holden, Harper Collins, 1996.
Collins Wild Guide: Wild Animals of Britain and Europe, John A. Burton, Harper Collins, 1998.
Eyewitness Handbooks: Trees, Allen J. Coombes, Dorling Kindersley, 1992.
Junior Nature Guides: Birds of Great Britain and Europe, Angela Royston, Dragon's World, 1995.
Junior Nature Guides: Wild Flowers of Great Britain and Europe, Pam Forey, Dragon's World, 1993.

Index